THE UGLY DUCKLING

A Puffin Easy-to-Read Classic

retold by Harriet Ziefert
illustrated by Emily Bolam

PUFFIN BOOKS

PUFFIN BOOKS
Published by the Penguin Group
Penguin Books USA Inc., 375 Hudson Street, New York, New York 10014, U.S.A.
Penguin Books Ltd, 27 Wrights Lane, London W8 5TZ, England
Penguin Books Australia Ltd, Ringwood, Victoria, Australia
Penguin Books Canada Ltd, 10 Alcorn Avenue, Toronto, Ontario, Canada M4V 3B2
Penguin Books (N.Z.) Ltd, 182–190 Wairau Road, Auckland 10, New Zealand
Penguin Books Ltd, Registered Offices: Harmondsworth, Middlesex, England

First published in the United States of America by Viking,
a division of Penguin Books USA Inc., 1997
Published simultaneously in Puffin Books

17 19 20 18

Text copyright © Harriet Ziefert, 1997
Illustrations copyright © Emily Bolam, 1997
All rights reserved

THE LIBRARY OF CONGRESS HAS CATALOGED THE VIKING EDITION AS FOLLOWS:
Ziefert, Harriet.
The Ugly Duckling / retold by Harriet Ziefert ; illustrated by Emily Bolam.
p.   cm. — (A Viking easy-to-read classic)
Summary: An ugly duckling spends an unhappy year ostracized by the other animals
before he grows into a beautiful swan.
[1. Fairy tales.] I. Bolam, Emily, ill. II. Andersen, H. C. (Hans Christian), 1805–1875. Grimme ælling.
III. Title. IV. Series.
PZ8.Z54Ug 1997   [E]—dc21 96–40056 CIP AC

Puffin Easy-to-Read ISBN 987-0-14-038352-2

Printed in U.S.A
Set in Bookman

Puffin® and Easy-to-Read® are registered trademarks of Penguin Books USA Inc.

Reading Level 1.6

THE UGLY
DUCKLING

Once upon a time,
nine ducklings hatched.

Eight were pretty
and fluffy and yellow.

But the ninth duckling
did not look like the others.

"You are not like the rest,"
said his mother.

"Ugly duckling! Ugly duckling!"
said the eight other ducklings.
"Ugly duckling! Ugly duckling!
Go away!"

The ugly duckling stayed away
from his eight brothers and sisters.

Once the mother duck took her ducklings
to visit another duck family
on the other side of the lake.

They teased the ugly duckling.
"You can't be a duck!
You can't be a duck!"

"I am a duck!
I am a duck! I am!"
cried the ugly duckling.

And then he ran away.

The ugly duckling hid in some grass.
Soon it got dark.

The ugly duckling was scared
and lonely.
He went to sleep.

The next morning, the ugly duckling
went to look for food.
"What kind of bird are you?"
asked some wild ducks.

"I am a duck," said the ugly duckling.

"You can't be a duck!
You can't be a duck!"
they teased.

The ugly duckling ran away
from the wild ducks.

He ran and ran until he came
to another lake.
"I'll stay here," he said.

The ugly duckling stayed all winter.
It was cold. Very cold.
And windy, too.

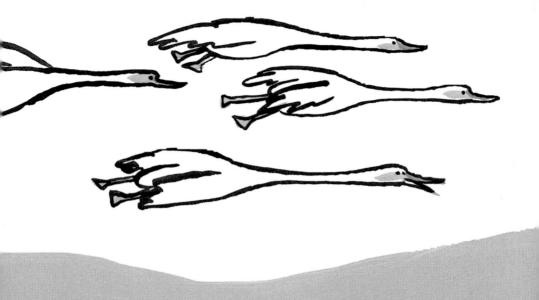

One day, the ugly duckling saw
some swans flying south.
"Come with us!" they called.

"I'm coming," cried the ugly duckling.
"Wait for me! Wait for me!"

The ugly duckling flapped his wings.
He tried to take off.
But he couldn't fly very well,
and the swans couldn't wait.

The ugly duckling stayed
by the lake.
He grew . . .

and grew . . .

and grew!

In the spring, the ugly duckling
flapped his wings.
They were big and strong.

"I can fly," he said.
"I can fly!"

He flew to a riverbank.
"Come and stay with us,"
said the swans.

"Who, me?" asked the ugly duckling.
"You don't want me.
    I'm just an ugly duckling."

"A duckling?" they said.

"No, you are a swan.
A beautiful swan, just like us!"